My Amazing Toddler
Behavioral Series

I Stay Calm.
I Wait My
TURN!

By
Suzanne T. Christian

TWORAVENS
BOOKS

Two Little Ravens
CHILDREN'S NON-FICTION BOOKS

Paperback Edition: 9781964202143
Hardcover Edition: 9781964202150
Digital Edition: 9781964202167

Published in the United States by Two Ravens Books LLC,
254 Chapman Rd, Ste 209, Newark DE 19702

'Expand the mind, free the imagination, one title at a time.'
www.tworavensbooks.com

Welcome to
"I Stay Calm.
I Wait My Turn!"

This book is filled with simple, engaging affirmations crafted especially for young children. As you read together, your toddler will learn the value of patience, self-control, and waiting their turn in everyday situations.

Each page of this book is a burst of color and joy, featuring bright, playful illustrations and relatable scenarios. This makes learning patience a fun and positive experience. By incorporating this book into your regular reading routine, you'll notice your child gradually developing stronger social skills, as the repetition of these affirmations helps them practice and grow.

Get ready for a joyful journey of patience, calmness, and emotional growth with your little one!

Suzanne T. Christian

I can wait,
and that's okay!

I stay calm like
a big tree.

When I wait,
I breathe in,
then out.
I am calm!

I can hop like a bunny while I wait!

It's fun to watch while I wait.

It's not my turn yet,
but I can smile!

Being patient is like waiting for yummy cookies to bake!

Even if I don't get my way, I stay calm and smile.

I'm a good friend
when I wait my turn.

When I wait, I can hum a little song.

Sometimes I don't get what I want and that's okay.

When I wait, I see what my friends do.

While I wait, I can wiggle my toes!

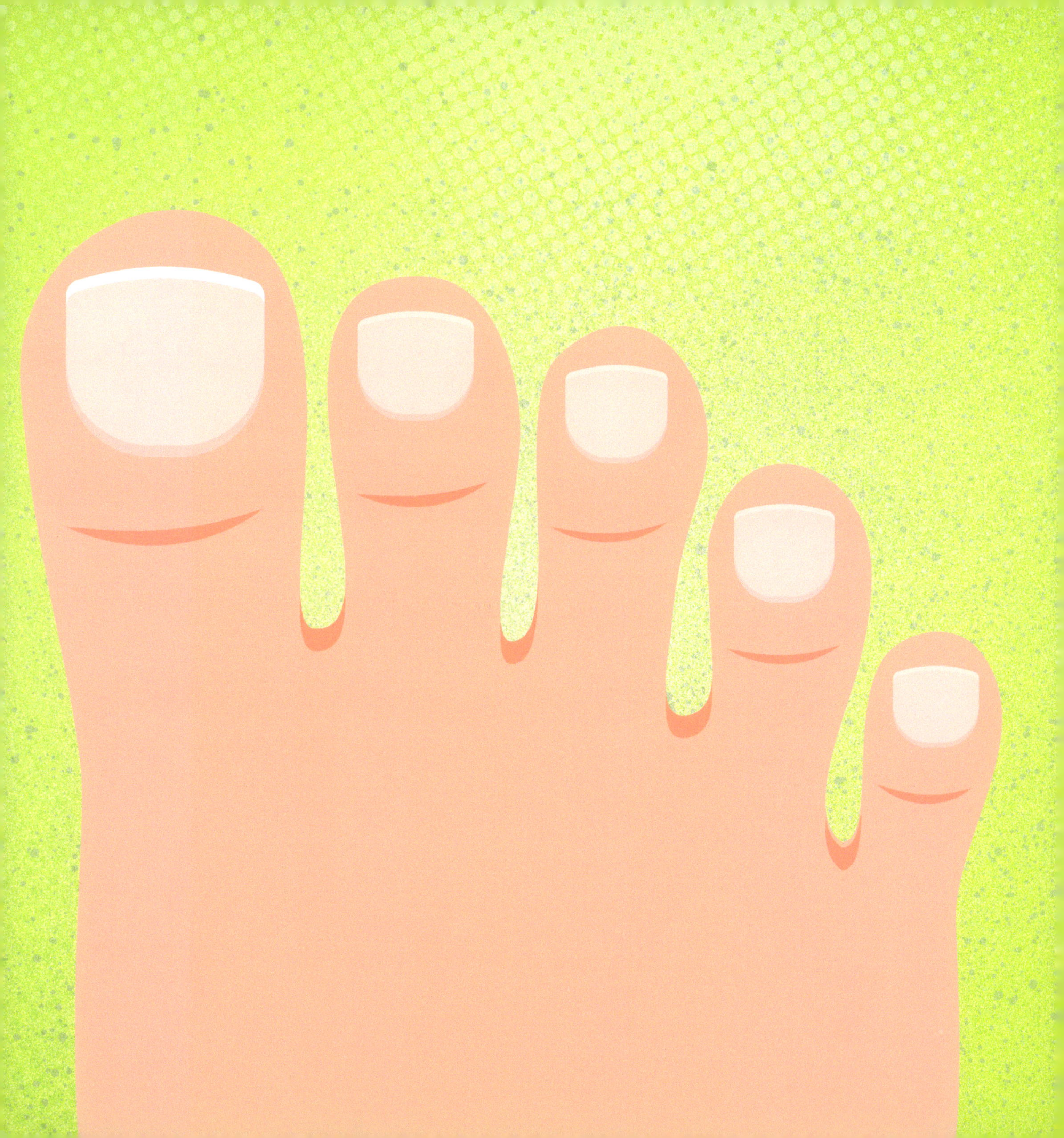

I stand in line, and
then I get to play.
I wait my turn!

When I wait, I'm like a quiet cloud.

If I don't get to play,
I can cheer for my
friends!

Waiting shows
I'm a kind friend.

Sometimes I wait, and that's
practice for next time.

Even if things don't go my way, I still stay calm.

I know I'll get my turn,
and I'm okay with that!

I can count
while I wait.

I stay calm.
I wait my turn!
The End!

My Amazing Toddler Behavioral Series

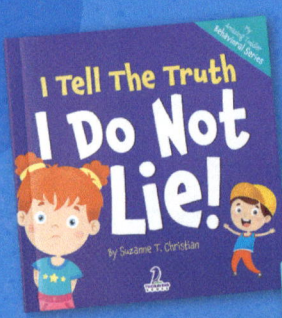

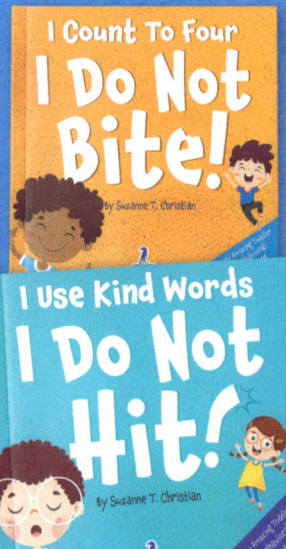

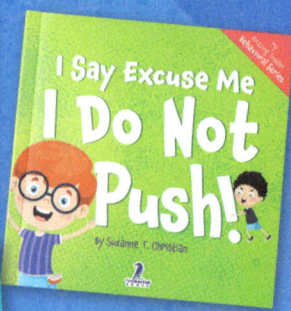

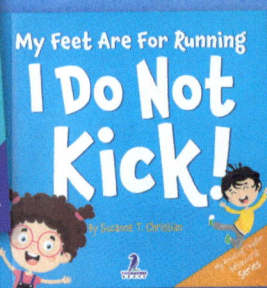

Check Out
Suzanne T. Christian's beloved series
'My Amazing Toddler Behavioral Series'.
Young readers are sure to enjoy!

Two Little Ravens
CHILDREN'S NON-FICTION BOOKS

Dear Amazing Reader,

Thank you for diving into **I Stay Calm. I Wait My Turn!** with me. If this book touched your heart or made a difference for a young reader, I'd be grateful if you could share your thoughts in a review. Your feedback inspires my future work and helps others discover the magic within these pages.

I'd love to hear from you directly if you have suggestions or ideas for improving the book. Please feel free to reach out to me at **suzanne.christian@tworavensbooks.com.** Your voice counts, and I cherish it deeply.

With heartfelt gratitude,